UP-POPS

paper engineering with elastic bands

Mark Hiner

The ten mechanisms

1. Octahedron

2. Flip-step

3. Cube

4. Tetrahedron

5. Double pyramid

6. Bevelled prism

7. Flash card

8. Open container

9. Right prism

10. Signal arms

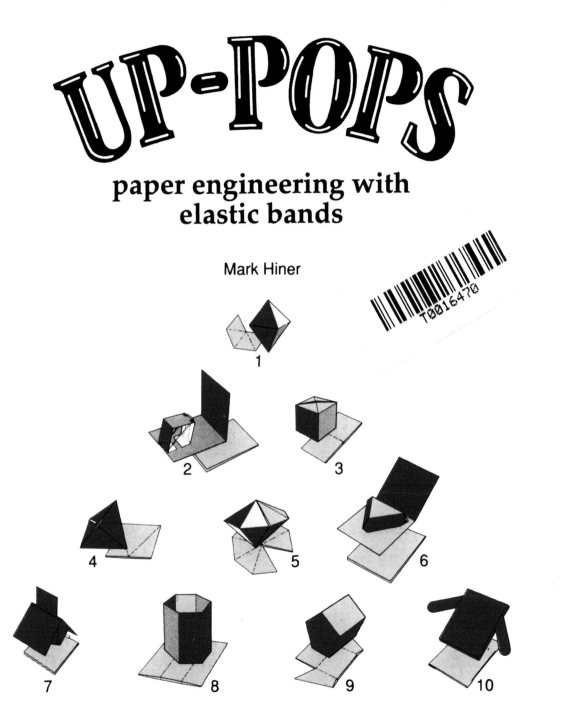

Tarquin Publications

What is an up-pop?

Most people have seen and been intrigued by the magic of pop-up books and there are certainly some wonderful ones being produced nowadays. They are not in fact a modern invention. True pop-up books were first published in England during the 17th century. Even earlier than that, books known as 'flap books' were produced. The main purpose of these was as medical text books, where the advantages of illustrating the anatomy of the body in successive layers could be appreciated by all. During the 19th and early 20th centuries, the production of pop-up books for children gradually came to be dominated by German publishers, with Lothar Megandorfer being acknowledged as perhaps the greatest of all. In the last twenty years there has been another upsurge in interest, this time on a world-wide scale. Advances in accurate colour printing and cutting and creasing has allowed imaginative designs to surpass even what was achieved at the height of the German period.

In my book 'Paper Engineering', I explained many of the ingenious mechanisms which are used in pop-up books and cards. Now, in this title, I explain how to add an element of greater surprise. The use of elastic power to power pop-ups gives them a life of their own. Instead of slowly forming when the page is opened, many of them almost explode into life as they are released from their envelopes or constraints.

It is these elastic powered pop-ups that we call UP-POPS.

M.H.

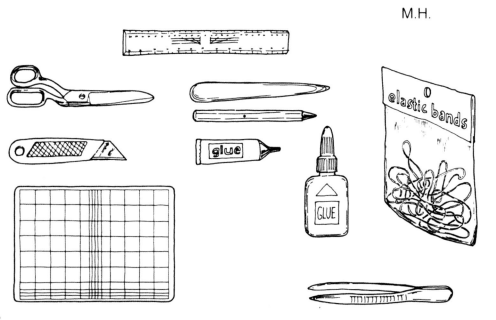

General Instructions

The design and construction of up-pop mechanisms is essentially a form of paper engineering with the addition of elastic bands. As with any kind of paper model work, there are certain tools and skills which are essential. The illustration below may serve as a reminder of what is required.

Cutting

Scissors are useful for cutting out the shapes roughly but always try to use a good sharp craft knife for the final cut. (Be sure the craft knife blade is very sharp to avoid the paper tearing whilst it is being cut.) Ideally, all the straight lines should be cut by drawing the knife along the edge of a metal ruler. This gives a good, clean, sharp edge to the model, however, curved lines (like around the hook) have to be cut freehand.

If you are using a craft knife make sure you use a cutting mat of some sort to protect the working surface. Expensive professional cutting mats are available from good art shops but a thick piece of card such as the back of a sketch pad should suffice.

Scoring

Successful paper engineering needs creases and folds which are crisp and accurate. This means that the paper must be scored so that it folds precisely along the desired edges. The best method is to rule along the lines with a ball-point pen which is out of ink. Some people will feel happier with a scoring stylus or a blunt craft knife. The aim is to compress the fibres of the paper so that it will fold and flex easily, but not to cut right through.

Glueing

To get the best results you will need a glue which sets quickly but not instantly and which does not make dirty marks. We particularly recommend a petroleum based glue like UHU or Bostic Clear. Good results may also be obtained with white adhesive like Copydex or PVA.

Because of the force which the elastic can exert, it is essential to be patient and to allow the glue to dry properly before testing the mechanism. Leaving it under a heavy book for some hours is the ideal to be aimed at.

Elastic Bands

It is not economical to try to buy elastic bands of precisely the length needed for each mechanism, nor is it necessary. A simple overhand knot will shorten a band and if it seems desirable to cut and rejoin a band then a reef knot will usually hold well enough. It is best to buy a small bag containing a selection of different sizes, choosing natural brown ones in preference to brightly coloured ones because they are usually springier. A few experiments will determine the appropriate thickness of band which is best for the project in hand. Avoid packets which look old, because elastic does age and become tired if kept in stock too long.

Making the models

Each of the ten working models in this book illustrates a basic up-pop mechanism. Follow these instructions step by step until each model is complete.

When the whole set has been made and has been stored within the book, the collection becomes a useful resource and a reference of possibilities within this branch of paper engineering.

1

Cut out all the pieces for the chosen mechanism from the central pull-out section, keeping well away from the outline.

2

Score along all score lines. Cut out all pieces precisely using scissors or a craft knife. Do not be tempted to cut along straight edges without using a metal ruler as a guide. A cutting mat is a useful asset.

3

Glue the pieces together in the order shown in the illustration, taking particular care over the hooks for the elastic bands.

Only cut out the hook and the slot once the glue is thoroughly dry.

4

● E ●

The elastic band is best fixed at a certain stage in the assembly.

At this stage the elastic band can be adjusted for length. As a reminder of the deadline for fitting the elastic band, all flaps which have to be glued later are marked with two dots. If you miss that time, you may need tweezers to fit the band.

5

Glue the restraining band for each mechanism on to its appropriate page.

6

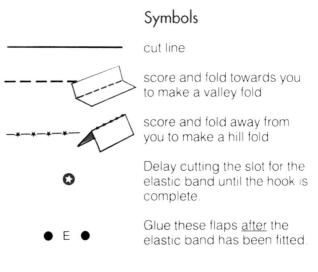

When the mechanism is fully assembled and works properly, store it within its band until it is required.

Symbols

—————————— cut line

- - - - - - - score and fold towards you to make a valley fold

-×-×-×-×- score and fold away from you to make a hill fold

✪ Delay cutting the slot for the elastic band until the hook is complete.

● E ● Glue these flaps <u>after</u> the elastic band has been fitted.

Designing your own up-pops.

The ten mechanisms in this book set out the basic ground rules for successful up-pop designs. Each can be regarded as a starting point for a whole range of interesting possibilities. Develop them for your own needs to express an idea, send a message or advertise a product in an inventive and individual way. Surprise people by sending out an unusual greetings card or an imaginative party invitation.

The right stuff.

Try to find a good art shop or graphic artists supplier which stocks a wide range of different cards and boards, as the material you use is rather important. Some cards are naturally much stiffer than others and stiffness is a particularly important property for up-pop mechanisms. The material used for the mechanisms in this book is 240gsm Chromocard and you will have noticed that it has a shiny side and a dull side. For the same grammage or weight two-sided card is rather weaker than this material and so it will be necessary to go to 280gsm or 300gsm. It is seldom wise to go for heavier weights than this because it becomes difficult to get clean folds. Indeed very thick material may even split apart when it is flexed. Usually only a few parts have to resist the pressure of the elastic and it is a sound strategy to double the thickness at a few selected places, rather than make the whole device too thick and clumsy.

The size that you make your up-pop mechanism is actually rather important. Do not try to make them too small. There is a sort of optimum size where the card is thick enough to withstand the stress of the elastic band and yet is thin enough to be still flexible. It is also apparent that larger mechanisms are much less awkward to assemble.

The right idea

It is not easy to consider all the problems associated with a new idea at the same time. It is best, therefore, to start by making a rough dummy and to use this dummy to see if the idea will work. Masking tape or clear tape can be handy to hold it together for a few trials. However, it should not be used for the final version, as it looks very messy and unprofessional.

Any decorations or drawings are much easier to do before the mechanism is glued together, but if you have second thoughts, at least all up-pop mechanisms will press flat and can be worked on then, one side at a time. Water-based paints may weaken the fibres and leave a crinkled surface and wax crayons may prevent the glue sticking, but there is no shortage of alternative materials to experiment with.

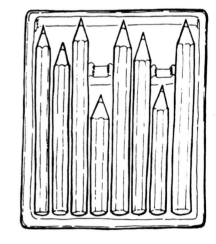

The right restraint

The essential element of an up-pop mechanism is that it jumps suddenly from a two-dimensional form into a three-dimensional form when it is released from its restraint. The design of the restraint is an integral part of the mechanism as a whole. The examples in this book demonstrate the effectiveness of a single band, but you may well prefer to use an envelope for your own design. If the intention is surprise, then perhaps using an ordinary commercial envelope might offer an advantage over making one specially. In which case, it is not a difficult task to determine the size of the finished mechanism by the need for it to fit snugly into a standard envelope.

Commercial applications.

Elasticated up-pop mechanisms are seldom seen in traditional pop-up books for children and it is interesting to consider why this should be. Most pop-up books nowadays are produced in countries like Colombia, Singapore and Hong Kong where labour is cheaper and where there is a tradition of quality printing and nimble handwork. Such books are produced in large quantities for world-wide distribution and editions are often produced in several different languages simply by changing the text plates as the printing continues. By such means can the costs of production and assembly be brought down and wonderful books can be produced for sale at a cost which is acceptable to the final consumer.

The addition of elastic power at certain stages of the production process would not present an insuperable problem, but it would add to the cost. For a sufficiently ingenious and appropriate application this cost might well be thought acceptable, but it has not generally been done. Perhaps the explanation lies in the length of the distribution chain and the fact that elastic does eventually perish. With the need to print and produce several years' supply at a time, there is perhaps the fear that the bands would have perished by the time they reach the final customer. Alternatively, and more positively, it may be that no first-class designer has yet come forward with a book so good that these difficulties will be accepted and overcome. Opportunities often come disguised as hard work and solutions to tricky problems, so perhaps we shall soon see the first examples of these up-pop mechanisms being used in imaginative children's books.

At present, the main applications are in business to business advertising. These elasticated up-pop mechanisms are used for publicity mailers because their dramatic, surprising action draws attention amidst an avalanche of junk mail. The cost of even the most imaginative up-pop mailer is very small indeed, set against the sale of an expensive computer or large capital item. Such mailers are usually produced in the home country in relatively small quantities for immediate use. Because of the particular problems of production, most up-pops are produced by specialist printers who have the necessary expertise in both printing and die-cutting and who also have a large workforce to assemble the up-pops.

Another modern trend which would appear to offer opportunities to up-pop designers is the increasing production and sale of expensive greetings cards. Customers are willing to pay surprising sums of money for a single card to mark some special occasion or event. Since many of these cards are already humorous and gimmicky, it would seem an ideal field for imaginative up-pop ideas.

Mechanism 1
Octahedron

This is an especially pleasing up-pop mechanism because all the folds are along its natural edges. It jumps into a symmetrical shape with a satisfying "snap" and forms the basis for many designs using biting teeth or snapping jaws.

GLUE BAND FOR MECHANISM 1 HERE.

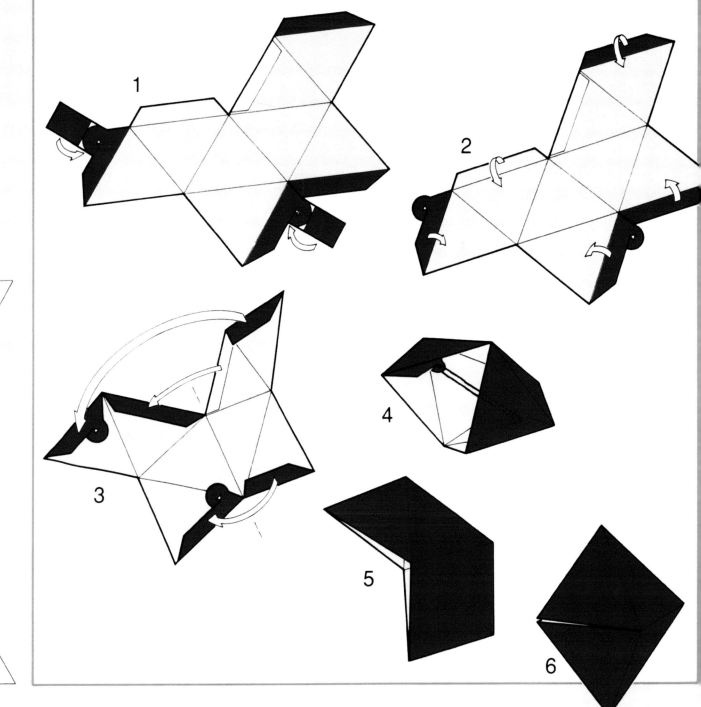

Mechanism 2
Flip-step

This mechanism does not generate a solid form, but it does offer a strong element of surprise. It rests passively within its protective card until it is opened sufficiently far. Then the step flips forwards and outwards in a sudden sharp movement.

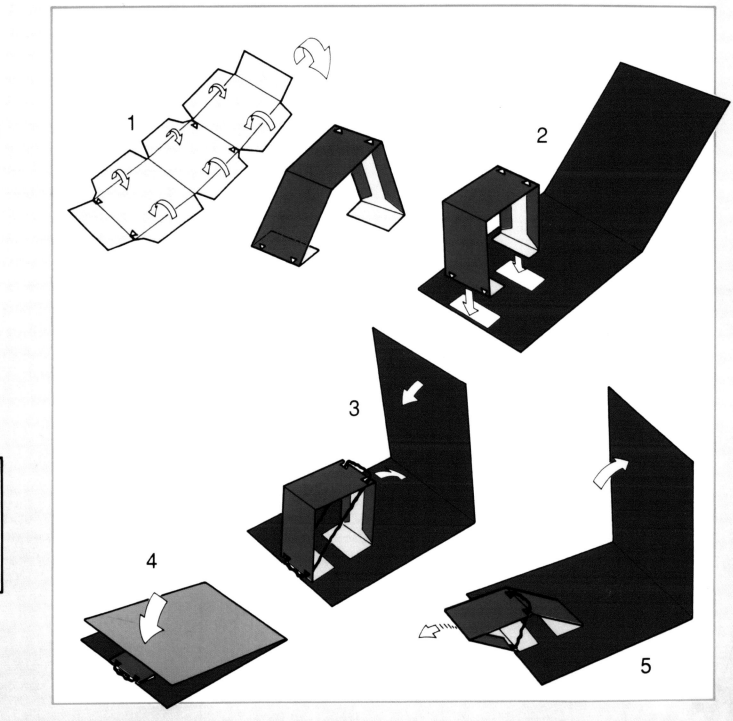

▲   ▲

GLUE BAND FOR MECHANISM 2 HERE.

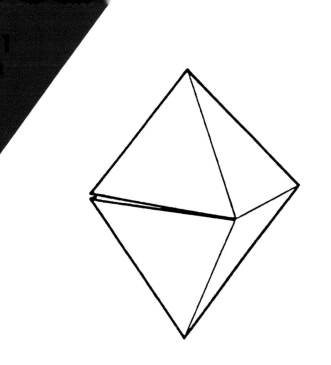

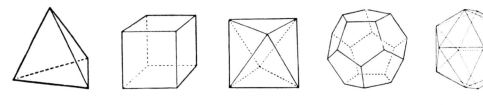

| Tetrahedron | Cube | Octahedron | Dodecahedron | Icosahedron |

The octahedron is one of the five fundamental polyhedra called the Platonic Solids. Each has all its faces the same regular polygon and all its edges are the same length. The octahedron is the only one of these solids which can be made as an up-pop without having folds or cuts across any of its faces. An interesting project is to construct a complete set of up-pop Platonic Solids to your own design.

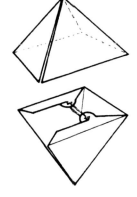

An alternative way of looking at this shape is to regard it as two pyramids with square bases which are joined together. There are other members of this family of double pyramids where the base is a pentagon, hexagon, heptagon etc. Mechanism 5 is another member of this family.

All the edges of an octahedron are equal and so each face is an equilateral triangle. Although the net can be drawn so that the mechanism can be constructed out of a single sheet of paper, it is probably more natural to think of it as a mechanism made out of two pieces.

Each piece consists of four sectors from a hexagon.

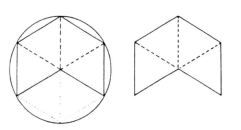

The hooks for the elastic bands should be opposite each other and be extensions of glue flaps. The other piece needs glue flaps on all four edges. This method of construction means that the edges which need extra strength have flaps of double thickness.

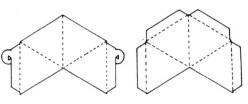

The shape of this mechanism suggests a mouth with biting teeth. However, don't make the mistake of putting both sets of teeth on the outside!

Send a Christmas card which can double-up as a tree decoration!

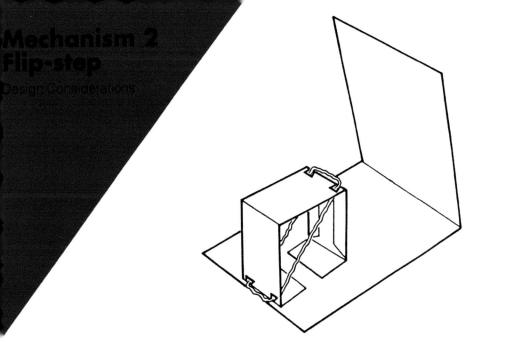

This mechanism is rather like a kind of reverse mousetrap. Its action would not catch a mouse but it could give an inquisitive rodent a sharp blow on the nose! More realistically, it can be primed to throw out a small shower of confetti. This might suggest designs for a card offering good wishes at a wedding.

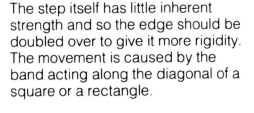

The easiest way to develop this mechanism is to add other layers of paper to the top or the front of the step. They can be of any shape as long as they are completely hidden when they are folded away inside the card.

The step itself has little inherent strength and so the edge should be doubled over to give it more rigidity. The movement is caused by the band acting along the diagonal of a square or a rectangle.

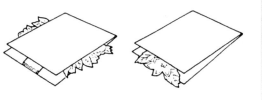

There is always a demand for a greetings card with an extra-special impact and this mechanism can form the basis for many original and interesting designs.

If the card is opened the other way, then it can be used for vertical, rather than horizontal, images.

Mechanism 3 Cube

This mechanism folds flat into a neat rectangular shape and then jumps up to form a cube, a shape normally associated with strength and solidity. The fact that its flattened shape is rectangular could well be important when looking for a design which is convenient to post in a standard envelope.

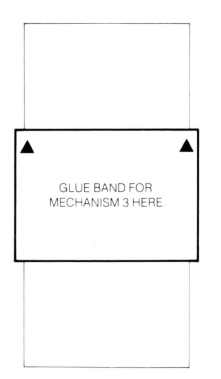

GLUE BAND FOR
MECHANISM 3 HERE.

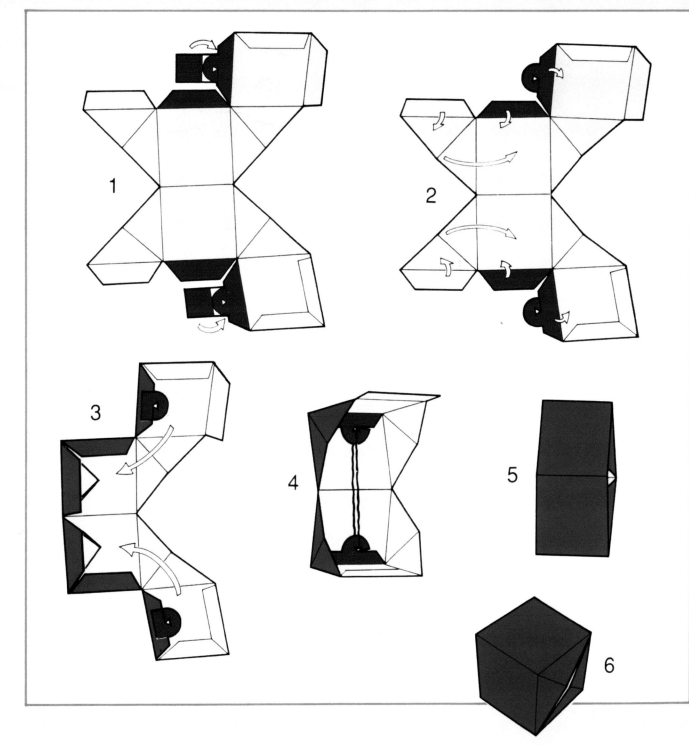

Mechanism 4
Tetrahedron

"If you have it, flaunt it" might well be the motto for this design. The elastic band is fully visible on the outside rather than being discreetly hidden inside as is commonly the case with up-pop mechanisms. Like the cube, the tetrahedron also jumps into its three-dimensional form from a rectangle.

▲   ▲

GLUE BAND FOR MECHANISM 4 HERE.

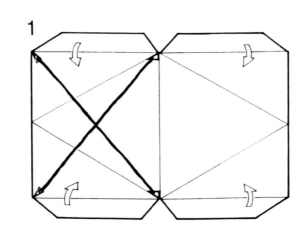

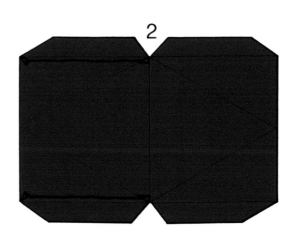

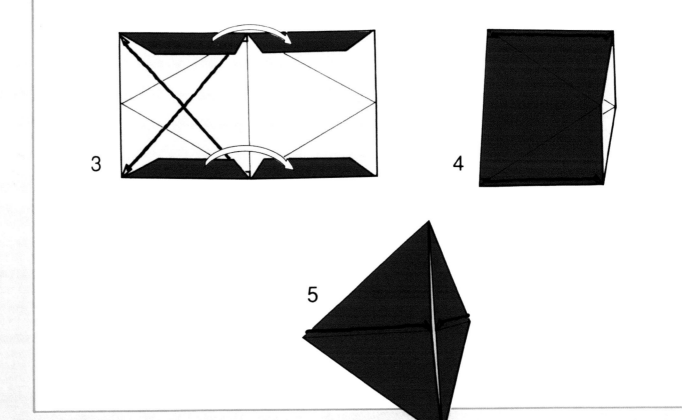

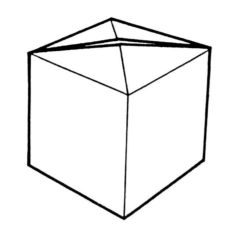

A cube is also a Platonic solid because its six faces are equal. However, to make it into an up-pop mechanism two of its faces must have cuts and folds along their diagonals. These cuts and folds lie parallel to each other on a pair of opposite faces.

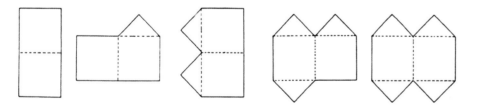

It is unusual to find a mechanism which can be flattened in so many different ways and yet still jump up into the same three-dimensional form. The flattened rectangle has obvious advantages, but some of the other formats might prove interesting for a particular application.

An envelope holding this mechanism tends to bulge. A band or holster seems preferable.

The cube is a special case of a cuboid where all the sides are equal. The cuboid, or rectangular box shape works perfectly satisfactorily as an up-pop mechanism.

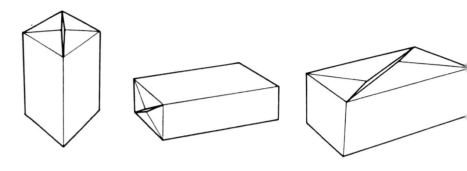

There are however, two additional points to note

(a) If the open ends are to fold inside the cuboid then the depth of the sides must be sufficient.

(b) When the edges of the opening faces are not equal, then the folds do not lie along the other diagonal. They each bisect the right angle.

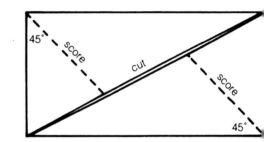

This mechanism lends itself to a favourite application called the "Magic Box". It is almost a conjuror's trick because not one, but two apparently solid cubes can be stored together and the smaller one appears to jump through a solid side. Remember to make the side of the smaller cube less than half the length of the side of the larger one.

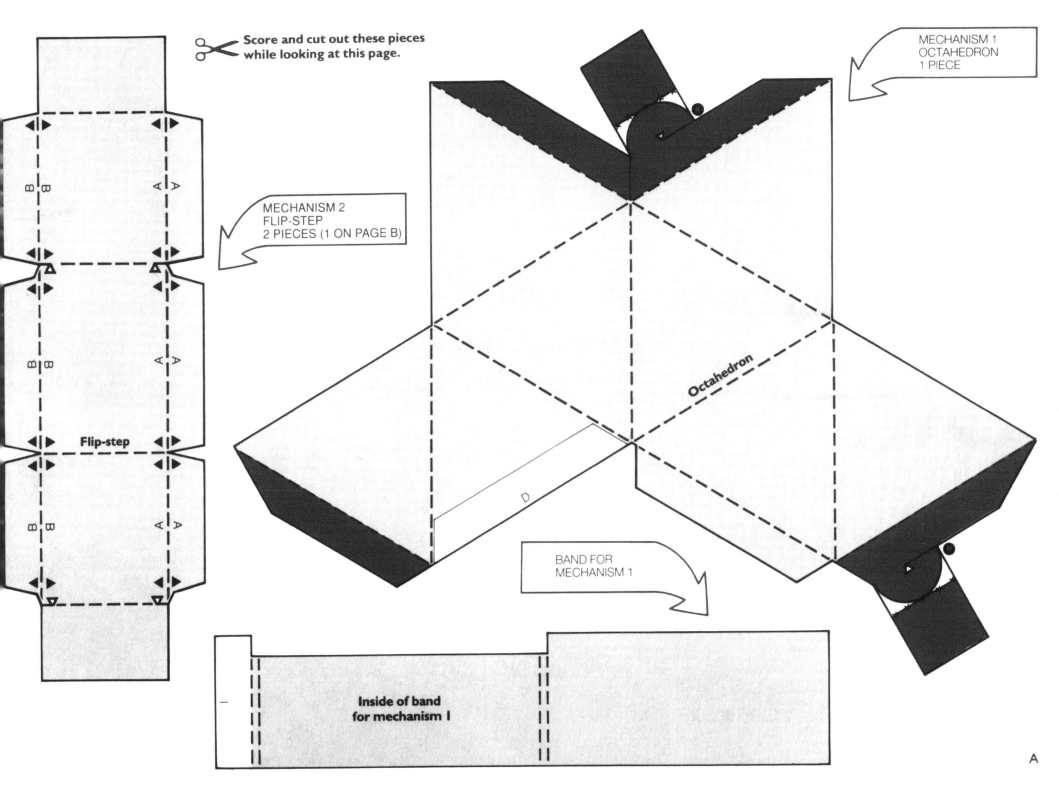

Score and cut out these pieces while looking at this page.

MECHANISM 1
OCTAHEDRON
1 PIECE

MECHANISM 2
FLIP-STEP
2 PIECES (1 ON PAGE B)

Octahedron

B B
A A

B B
A A

Flip-step

B B
A A

D

BAND FOR
MECHANISM 1

**Inside of band
for mechanism I**

A

Score and cut out these pieces while looking at the other side.

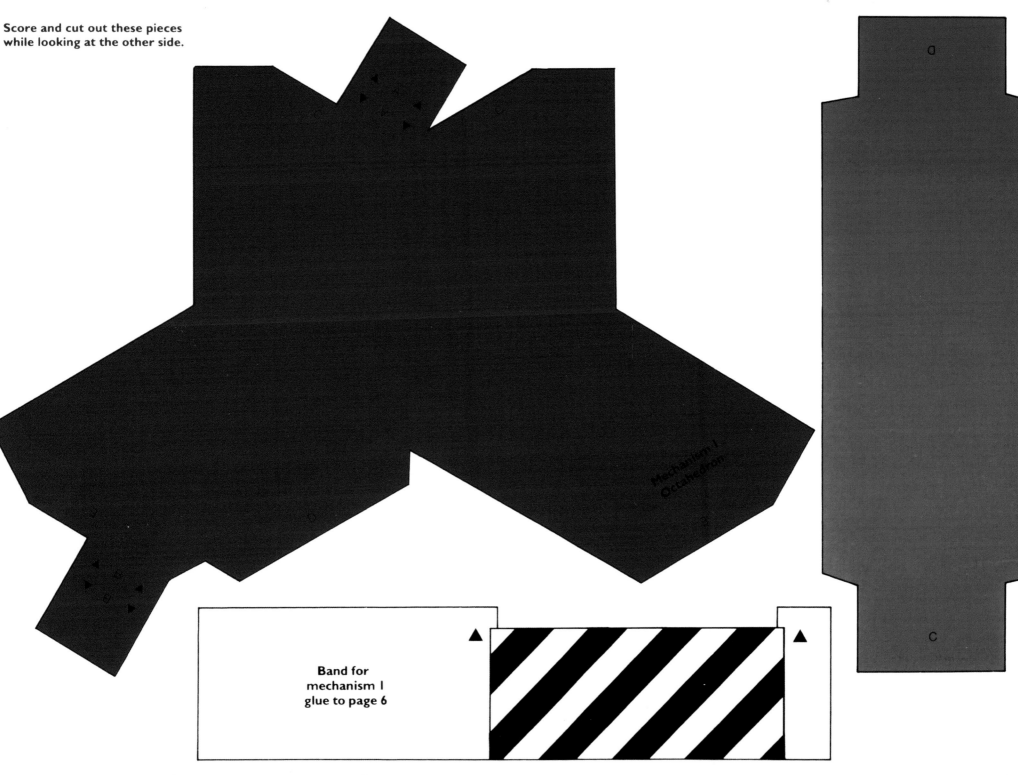

Mechanism I
Octahedron

Band for
mechanism I
glue to page 6

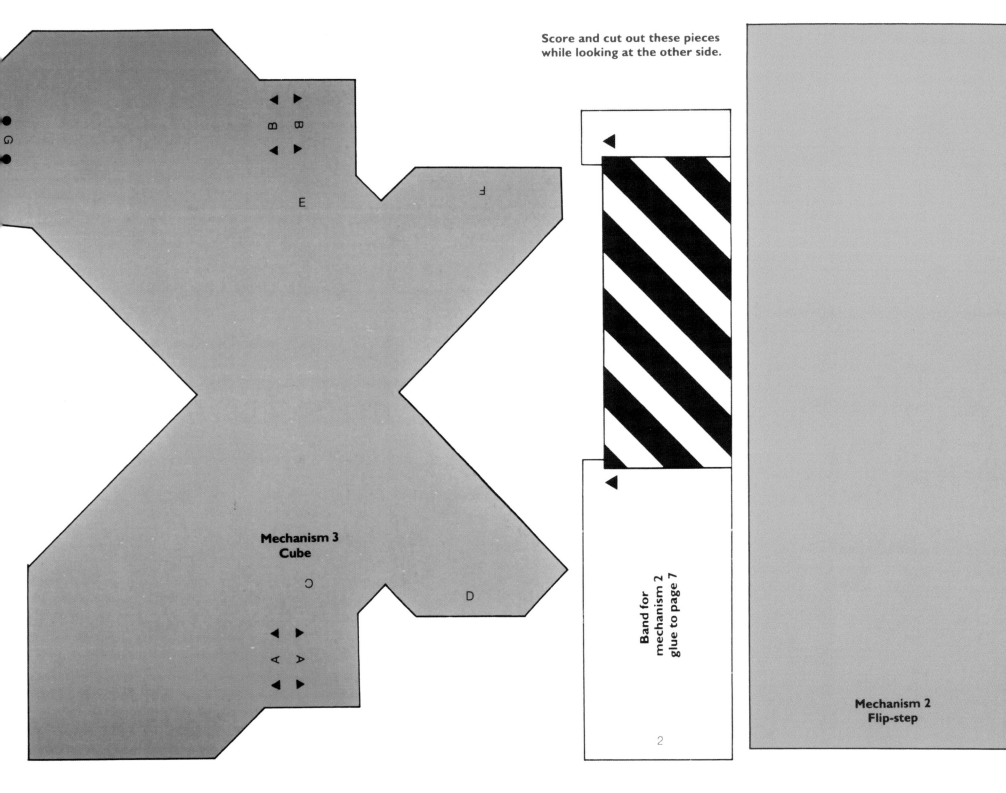

Score and cut out these pieces while looking at the other side.

G

B B

E

F

Mechanism 3
Cube

C

D

A A

Band for
mechanism 2
glue to page 7

2

Mechanism 2
Flip-step

C

D

Flip-step

MECHANISM 2
FLIP-STEP
2 PIECES (1 ON PAGE A)

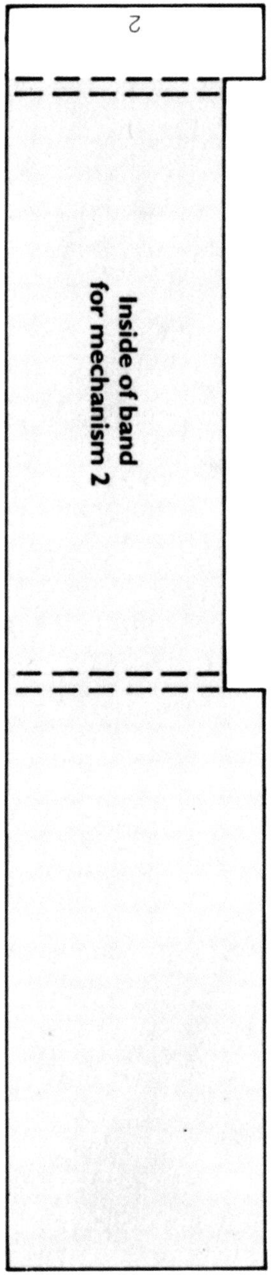

2

**Inside of band
for mechanism 2**

Cube

F

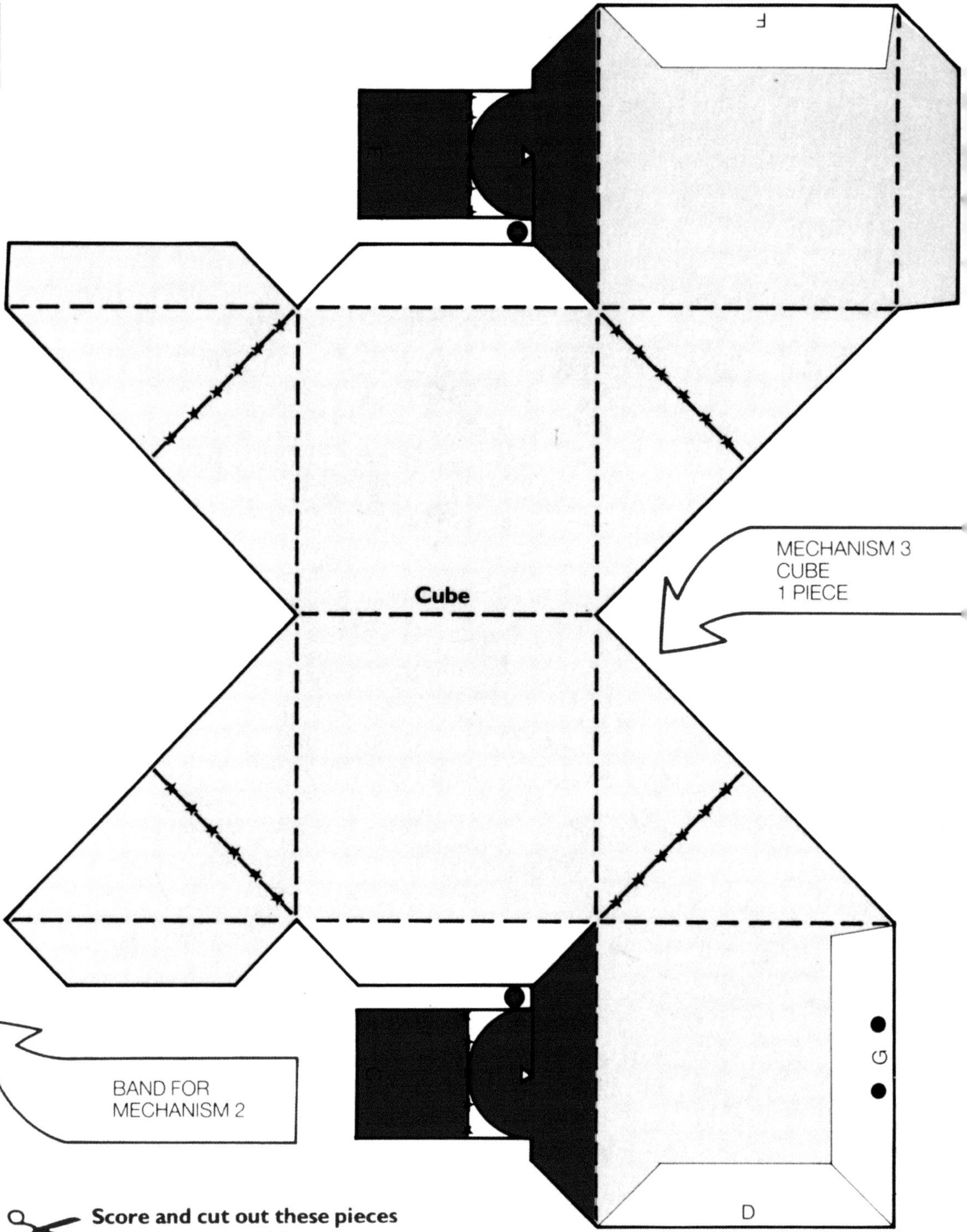

MECHANISM 3
CUBE
1 PIECE

G

D

BAND FOR
MECHANISM 2

✂ **Score and cut out these pieces
while looking at this page.**

B

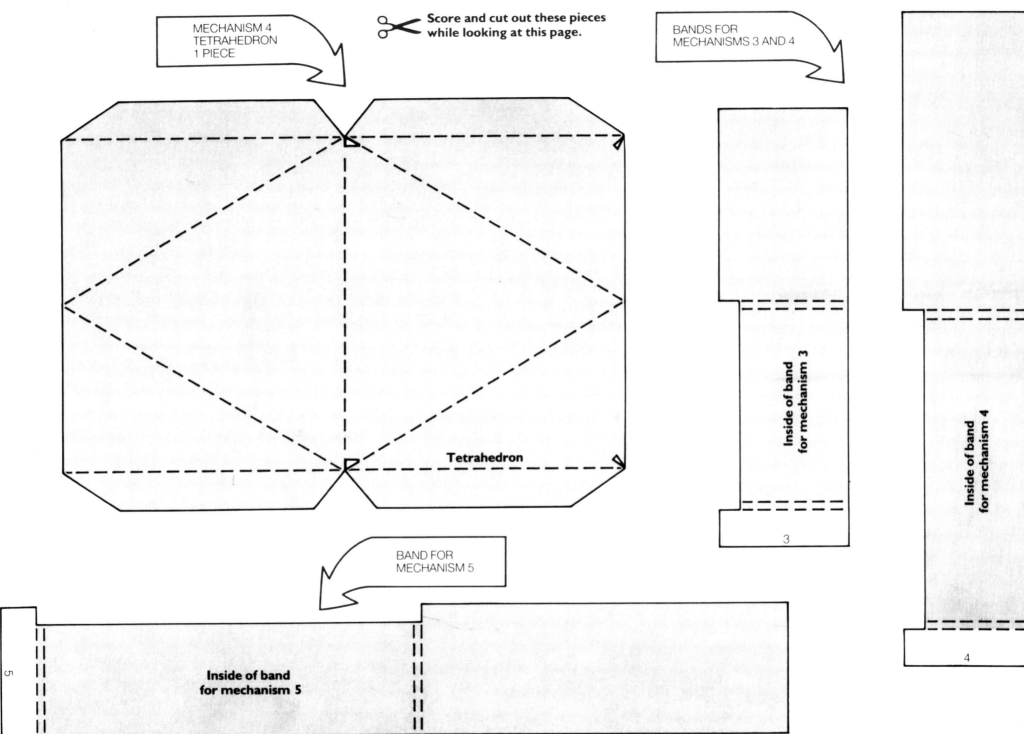

MECHANISM 4
TETRAHEDRON
1 PIECE

Score and cut out these pieces while looking at this page.

BANDS FOR MECHANISMS 3 AND 4

Tetrahedron

Inside of band for mechanism 3

3

BAND FOR MECHANISM 5

Inside of band for mechanism 5

5

Inside of band for mechanism 4

4

C

Score and cut out these pieces
while looking at the other side.

Band for
mechanism 4
glue to page 11

4

Band for
mechanism 3
glue to page 10

3

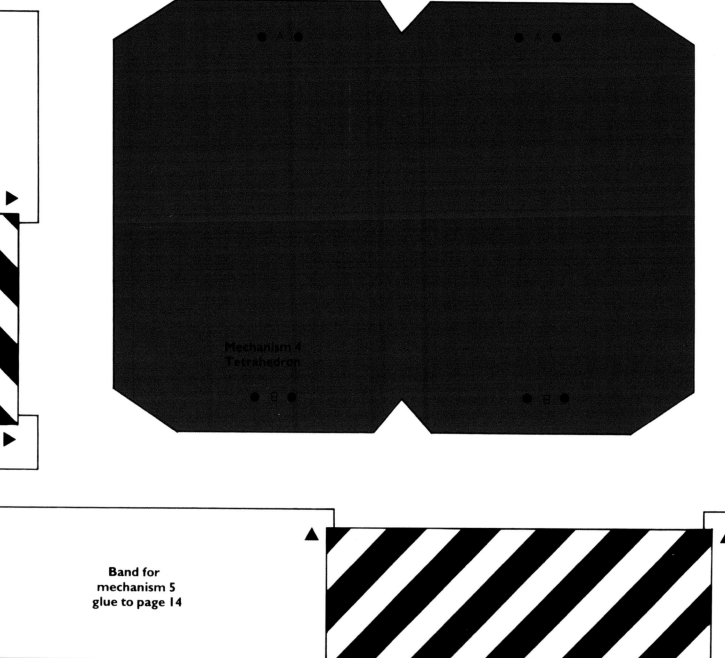

Mechanism 4
Tetrahedron

Band for
mechanism 5
glue to page 14

5

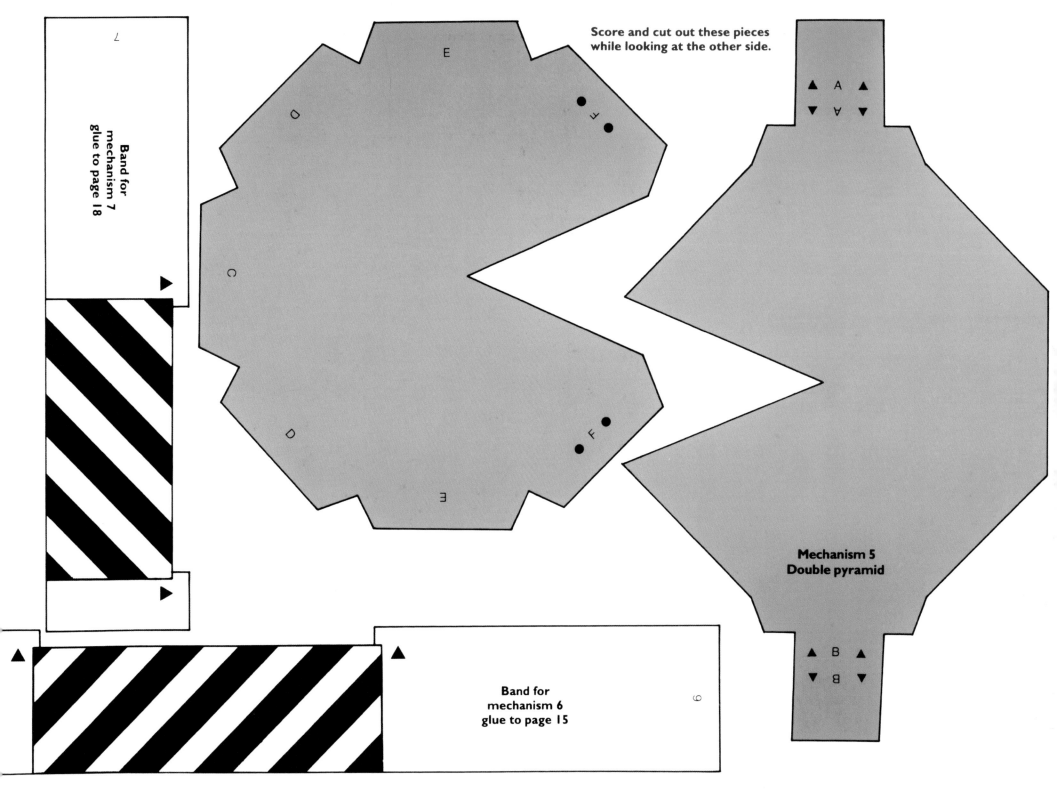

Score and cut out these pieces while looking at the other side.

Band for
mechanism 7
glue to page 18

7

Band for
mechanism 6
glue to page 15

Mechanism 5
Double pyramid

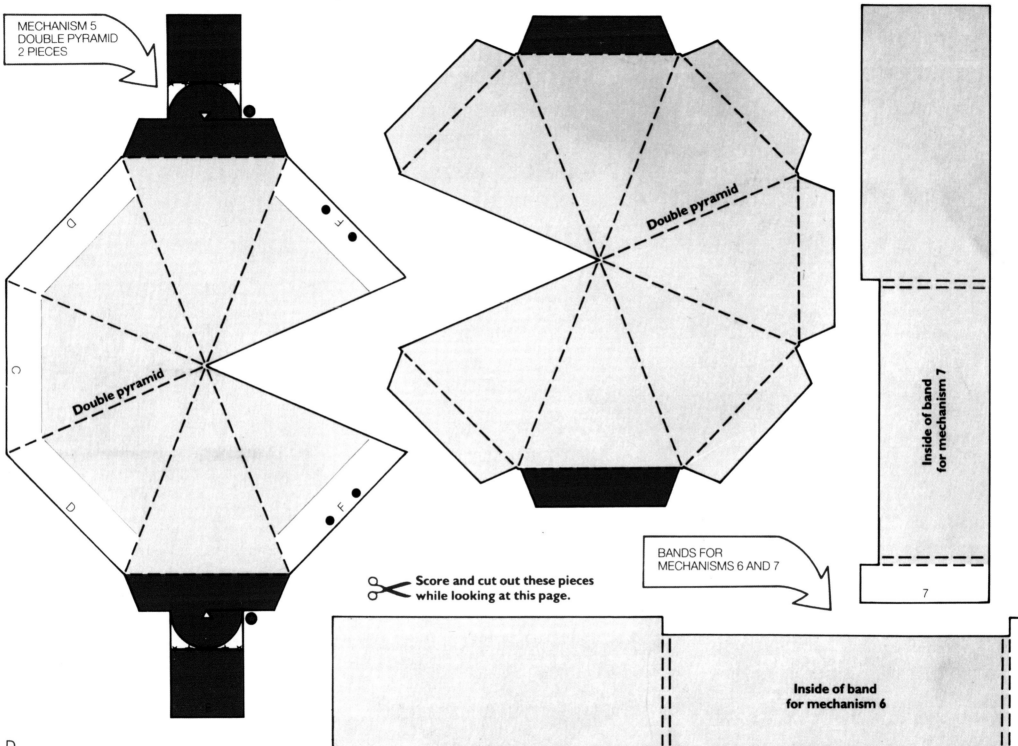

MECHANISM 5
DOUBLE PYRAMID
2 PIECES

Double pyramid

Double pyramid

Inside of band
for mechanism 7

7

BANDS FOR
MECHANISMS 6 AND 7

✂ **Score and cut out these pieces
✂ while looking at this page.**

**Inside of band
for mechanism 6**

6

D

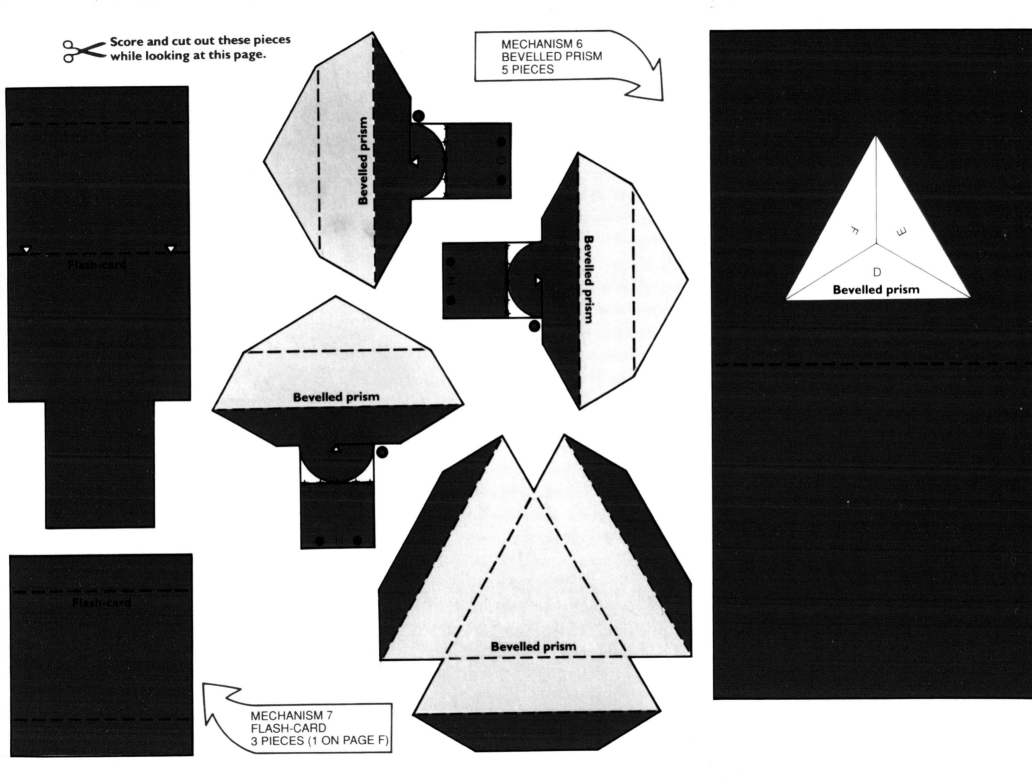

✂ **Score and cut out these pieces while looking at this page.**

MECHANISM 6
BEVELLED PRISM
5 PIECES

Bevelled prism

Bevelled prism

Bevelled prism

Bevelled prism

Bevelled prism

Flash-card

Flash-card

MECHANISM 7
FLASH-CARD
3 PIECES (1 ON PAGE F)

E

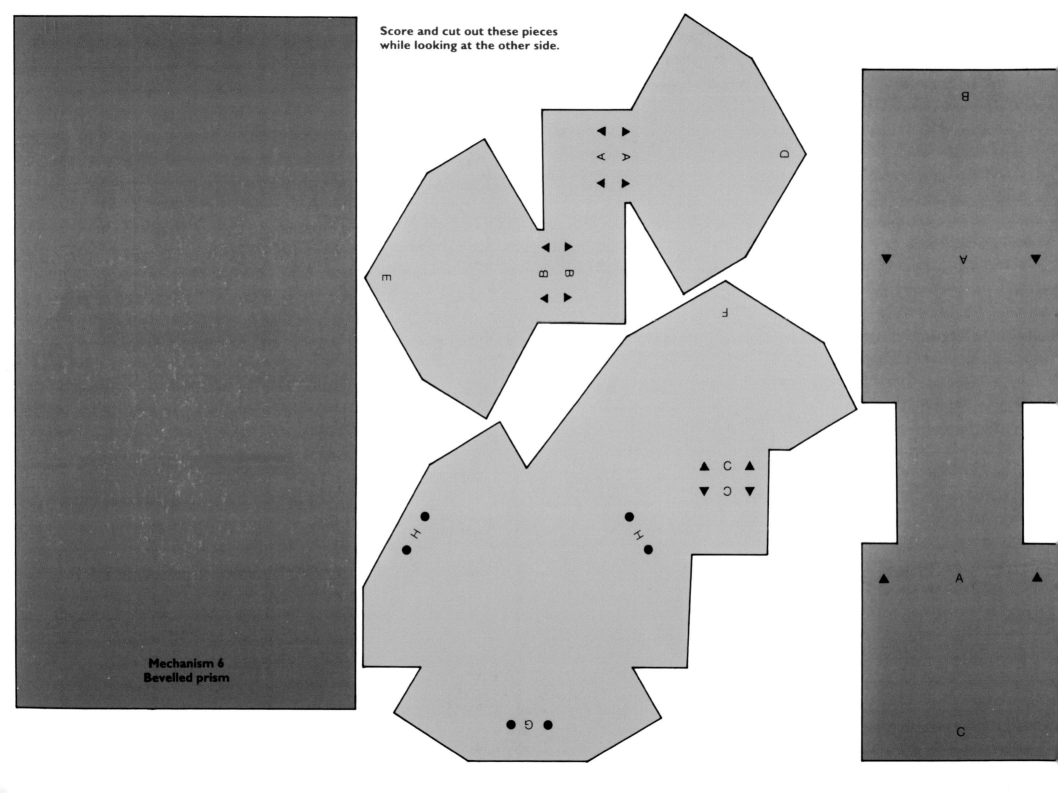

Score and cut out these pieces while looking at the other side.

Mechanism 6
Bevelled prism

Score and cut out these pieces
while looking at the other side.

Mechanism 8
Open container

Mechanism 7
Flash-card

Band for
mechanism 8
glue to page 19

8

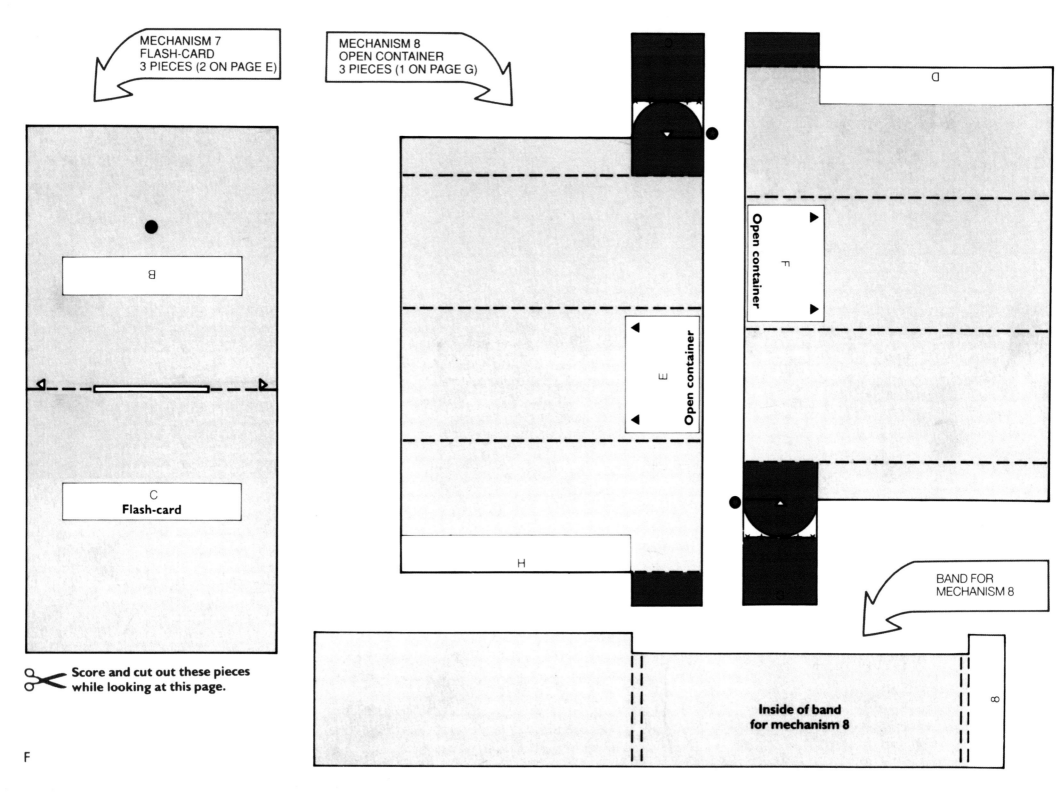

MECHANISM 7
FLASH-CARD
3 PIECES (2 ON PAGE E)

MECHANISM 8
OPEN CONTAINER
3 PIECES (1 ON PAGE G)

B

C
Flash-card

Open container
E

Open container
F

D

H

BAND FOR
MECHANISM 8

**Inside of band
for mechanism 8**

8

✂ **Score and cut out these pieces
while looking at this page.**

F

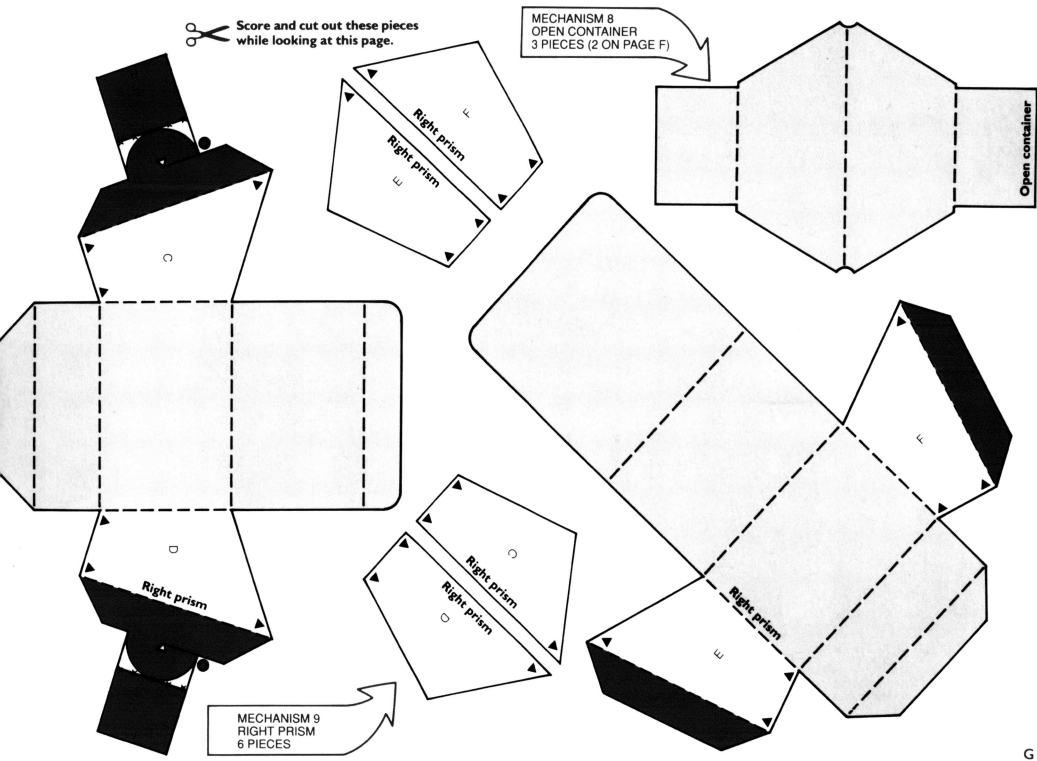

Score and cut out these pieces while looking at this page.

MECHANISM 8
OPEN CONTAINER
3 PIECES (2 ON PAGE F)

Open container

Right prism

Right prism

Right prism

Right prism

Right prism

Right prism

MECHANISM 9
RIGHT PRISM
6 PIECES

G

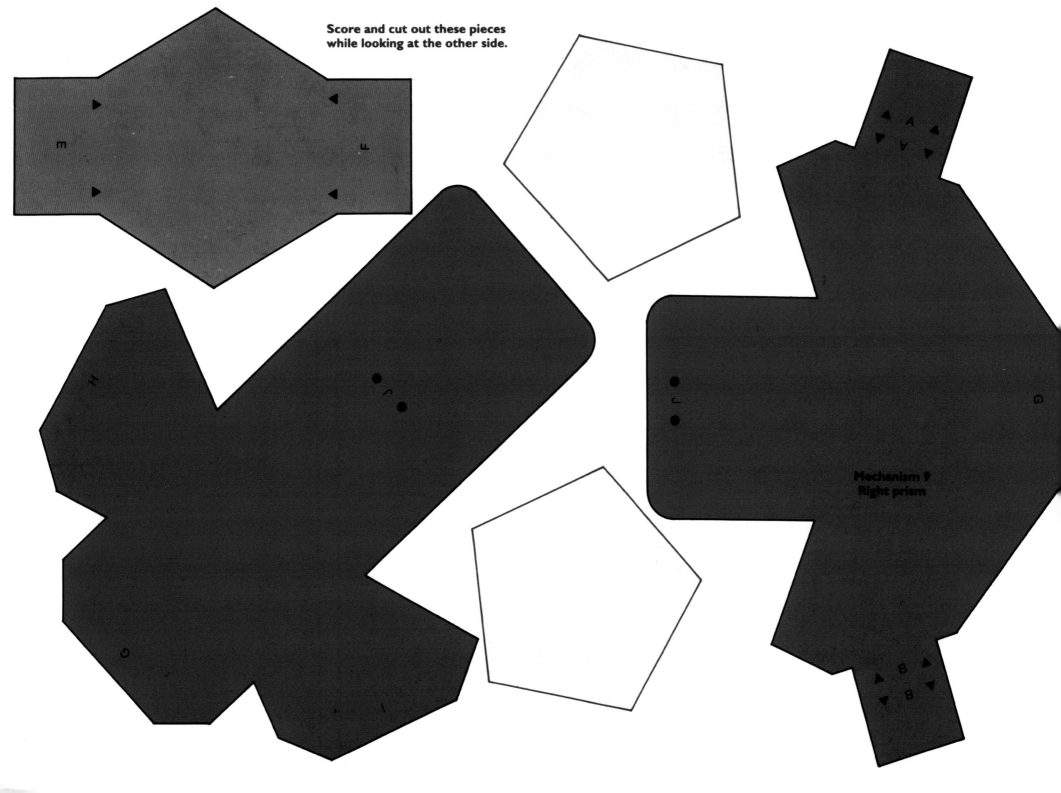

Score and cut out these pieces
while looking at the other side.

Mechanism 9
Right prism

Score and cut out these pieces
while looking at the other side.

B
B B
B

▲ **Band for
mechanism 9
glue to page 22**

9

▲ **Band for
mechanism 10
glue to page 23**

10

D
D D
D

F
F F
F

Mechanism 10
Signal arms

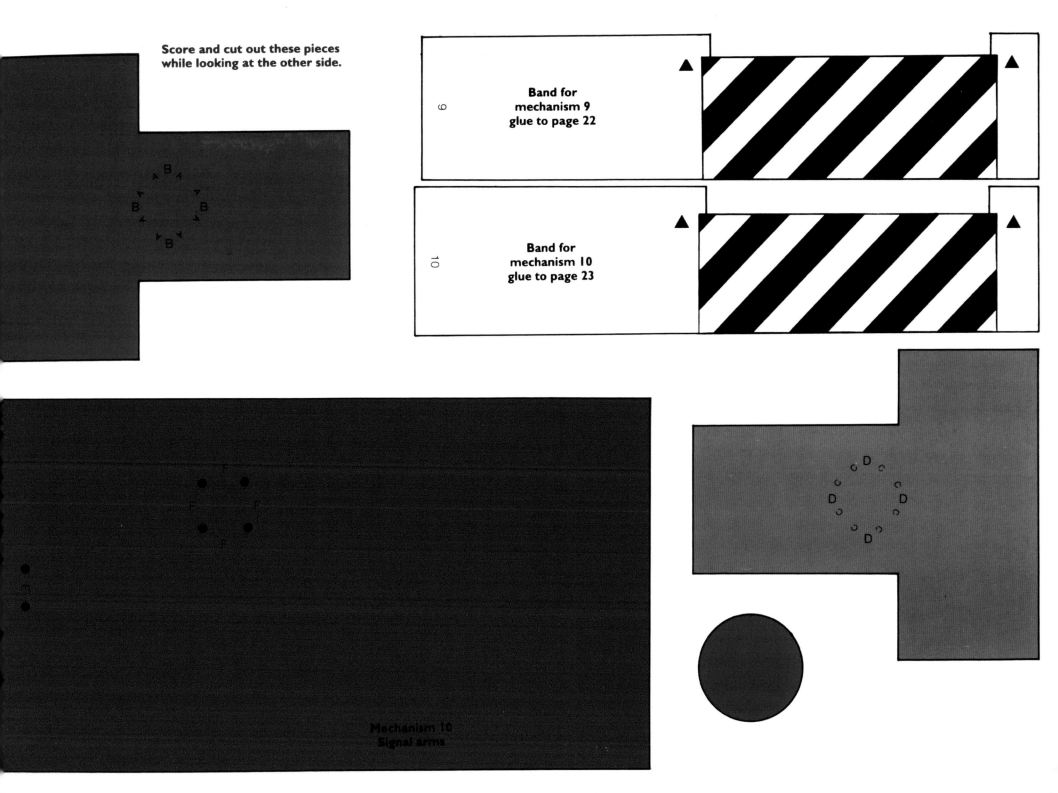

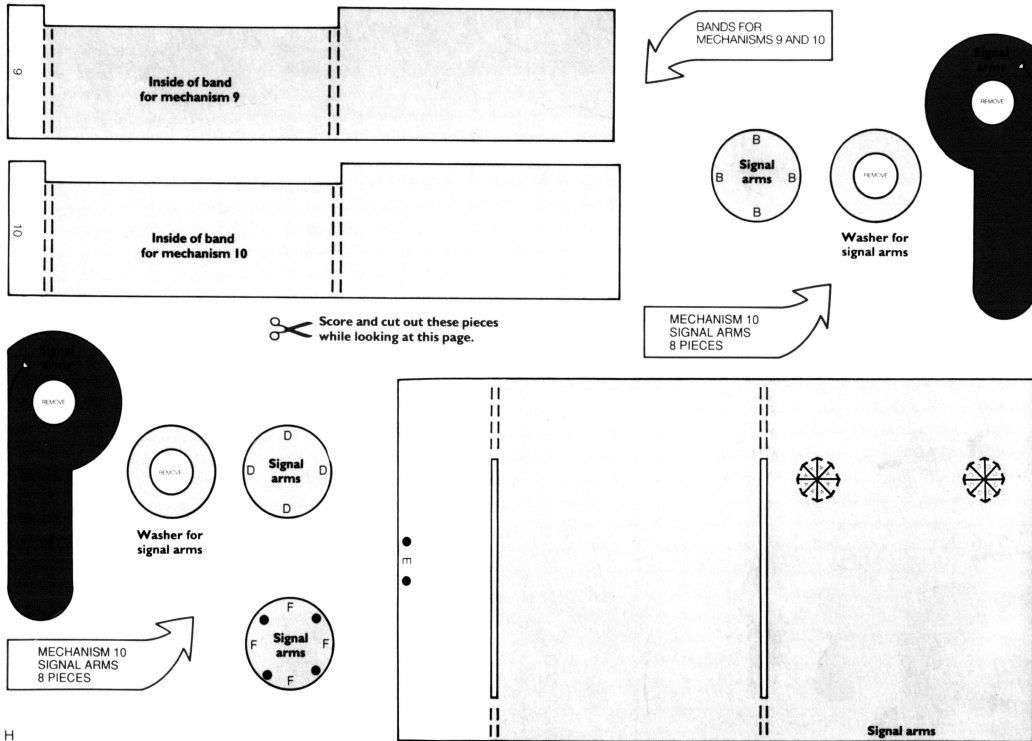

9

Inside of band
for mechanism 9

10

Inside of band
for mechanism 10

✂ Score and cut out these pieces
while looking at this page.

BANDS FOR
MECHANISMS 9 AND 10

Signal
arms

REMOVE

B
B Signal B
arms
B

REMOVE

Washer for
signal arms

MECHANISM 10
SIGNAL ARMS
8 PIECES

Signal
arms

REMOVE

REMOVE

D
D Signal D
arms
D

Washer for
signal arms

MECHANISM 10
SIGNAL ARMS
8 PIECES

F
F Signal F
arms
F

E

Signal arms

H

Mechanism 4
Tetrahedron
Design Considerations

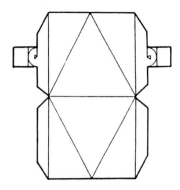

There is no reason why an up-pop tetrahedron has to have the elastic band on the outside. It can also be made with hooks and an internal band. Since it can be awkward to fix or replace the band, it is best not to make the tetrahedron too small.

Non-mathematicians might be surprised to find out that the angles for the glue flaps are neither 30° nor 60°, but about 35° and 55°. Examination of the three-dimensional form will show why. Getting them wrong is not too serious as they can easily be trimmed to fit by trial and error.

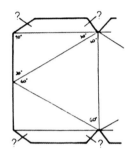

A tetrahedron is the simplest of the Platonic Solids, having fewer edges, faces or vertices than any other. However, it can only be made into an up-pop by having folds across two of its four faces.

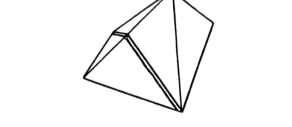

Having made one tetrahedron which pops-up, it can be seen that another identical one could be glued to it, solid face to solid face. The resulting shape will still fold flat and then up-pop successfully. Having made two, why not three or four? Experiment with different combinations.

Do the tetrahedra all have to be the same size?

Here are two design ideas which seem particularly suitable for a tetrahedron shape.

Mechanism 5
Double Pyramid

This mechanism is one of the most commonly used up-pop designs. It springs into its three-dimensional shape with a satisfying "snap" when it is released from its restraint. The net of each of the pyramids is a regular octagon with one sector removed, giving a heptagonal base to the double pyramid. It is a typical member of an up-pop family which offers many different possibilities.

▲ GLUE BAND FOR MECHANISM 5 HERE. ▲

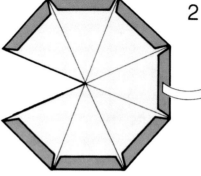

1

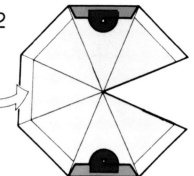

2

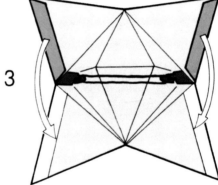

3

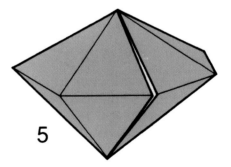

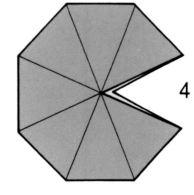

4

5

14

Mechanism 6
Bevelled Prism

This kind of up-pop is attractive because it produces a shape which looks solid but which has a curious springy feel when it is pressed. There is an additional element of puzzlement about this type of mechanism because it is not easy to look inside and see exactly how it works.

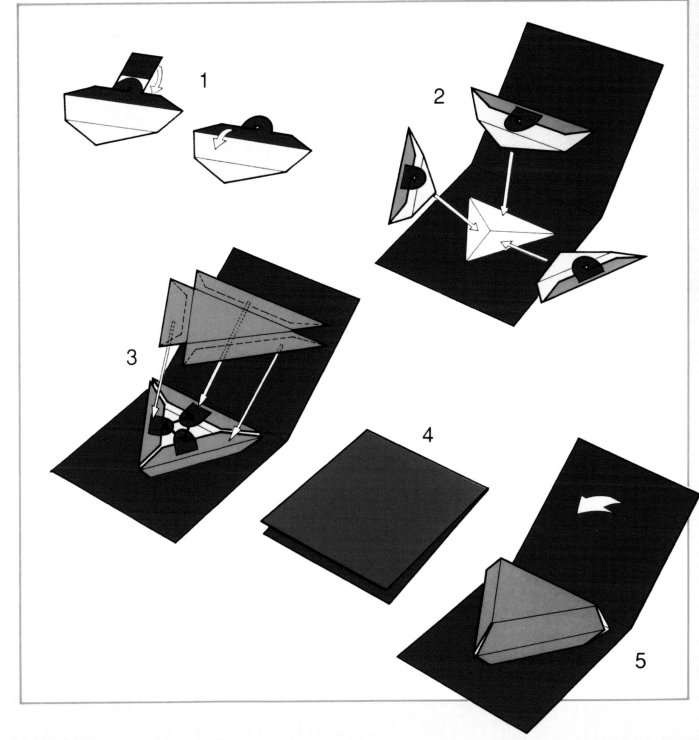

GLUE BAND FOR MECHANISM 6 HERE.

15

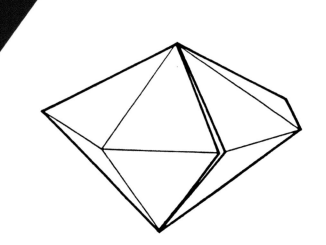

As with the octagon, leaving out 1, 2 or more sectors from other regular polygons gives a family of double pyramids with different numbers of sides and of different steepness. To some people these shapes may suggest crystals or jewels, perhaps also suggesting ideas for decoration.

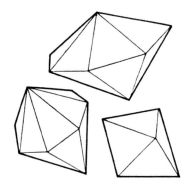

Since the most striking feature of this mechanism is the satisfying "snap" it makes as it is taken from its envelope, it may suggest designs for monsters, strange fish with biting teeth and extra-terrestrial lifeforms. Although many people may prefer to keep the shapes pure, there is no law to say that you cannot add strange tails, fins, eyes or tentacles if you wish.

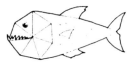

This mechanism belongs to the same family as mechanism 1, although this might not be immediately obvious to a casual observer. It is best to make it from two identical pieces, each obtained from a regular octagon. The easiest way to draw any regular polygon is to start with a circle.

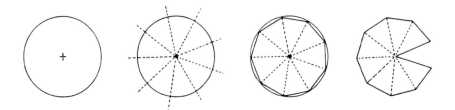

This diagram shows the method of construction. By leaving out one sector in each half, the double pyramid has 7 sides. If two sectors are left out of each half, then the resulting double pyramid will be steeper and have 6 sides. Then it is necessary to add the glue flaps and the hooks for the elastic bands.

Other members of the family can be constructed by changing the angle at the centre.

No. of sides of polygon	5	6	7	8	9	10
Angle at centre	72°	60°	51.4°	45°	40°	36°

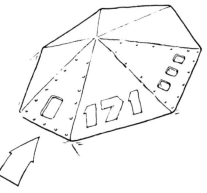

It also lends itself naturally to flying saucer designs. It will in fact fly quite well when thrown with a spin. For this purpose, the flatter the better.

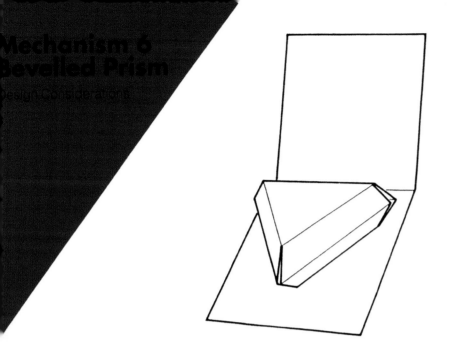

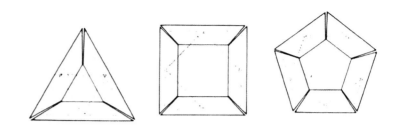

This diagram shows the first three members of this family with the elastic bands arranged to exact equal forces on all sides.

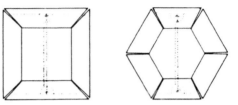

It is worth experimenting with both methods of fixing for the four-sided and six-sided versions.

This tricorn shape is the first in a natural series of up-pops which can either be enclosed in a card or made as free-standing forms. However many sides it has, the top and bottom planes must be parallel and the sides must be slightly convex so that they do not collapse inwards under the pressure of the elastic.

The six-sided member of this family is one which is of particular interest. Not only is it symmetrical, but having 12 sides in total, it lends itself naturally to use in calendar designs.

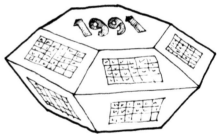

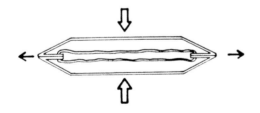

When the model is squashed flat the sides move outwards and the corners open. For shapes with an even number of sides the elastic can be stretched between hooks on opposite sides. Such a method becomes impossible for those with an odd number of sides.

This is its net using a straight elastic band. Notice how each half side is a trapezium to make sure that the opposite sides remain convex and cannot collapse inwards.

Mechanism 7
Flash-card

If the essential quality of an up-pop is surprise, then this one certainly has it. Not only does it spring open with a decisive "snap", but the mostly hidden tongue jumps out through a slit in its edge. Since the whole mechanism forms a stable stand, the message or image on either side of the flash-card cannot fail to demand attention.

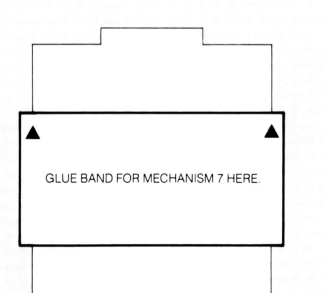

GLUE BAND FOR MECHANISM 7 HERE.

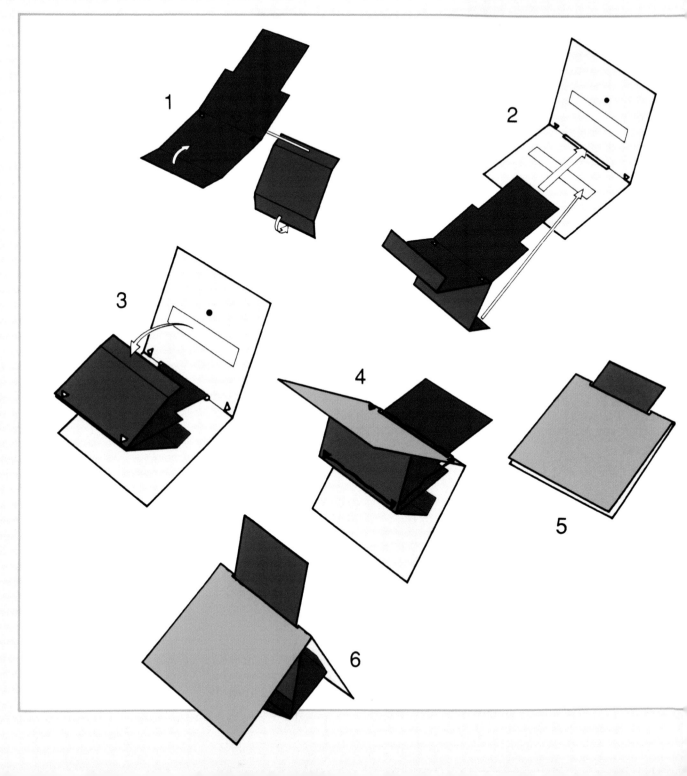

Mechanism 8
Open Container

This version of the open container mechanism is hexagonal in cross-section. It has a solid base and sufficient depth to hold pens and pencils making it a popular up-pop mechanism for business to business advertising. It is a particularly robust and reliable design.

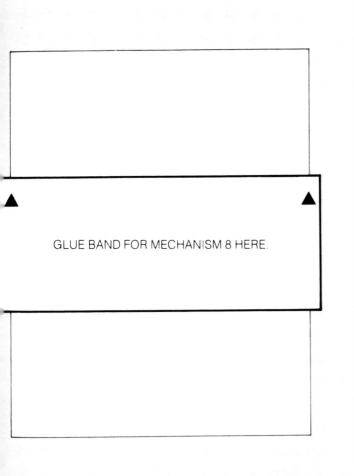

GLUE BAND FOR MECHANISM 8 HERE.

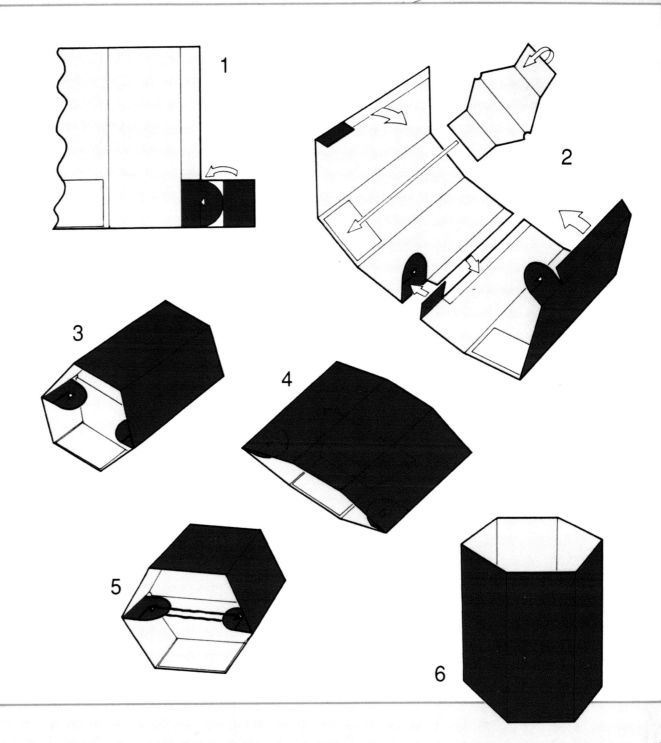

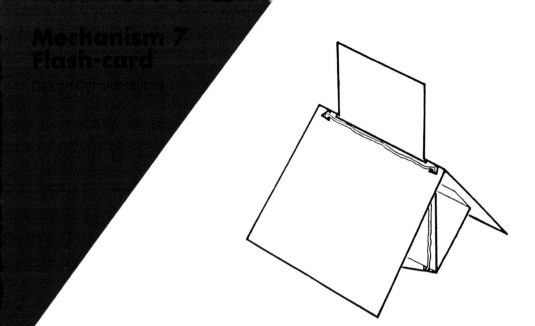

As with several other mechanisms, the motive force is provided by the elastic band pulling along the diagonal of a square. Two sides of the square are part of the card and the other two are glued to it. If the elastic band and the tongue were removed the square would fold flat both ways as the card was opened and closed.

The complete mechanism works by allowing the elastic power to shorten one diagonal so far, but no further. By putting shoulders on the tongue and arranging the lengths so that the elastic band never becomes slack, the card opens with a satisfactory snap and pushes out the tongue in a rapid motion. At the same time the half open card forms a convenient stand, a characteristic which has not been missed by many greetings card designers.

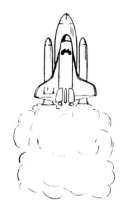

It is particularly pleasing to match the message with the messenger, or in this case the image with the mechanism.

It seems very appropriate to link the sudden appearance of the tongue with a rocket launch or the release of four and twenty blackbirds!

In the right circumstances, any of these ideas might also be appropriate images for a flash-card design.

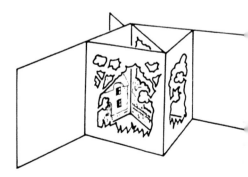

A true enthusiast might like to draw two more scenes inside the mechanism which can be seen via peep holes when the card is open.

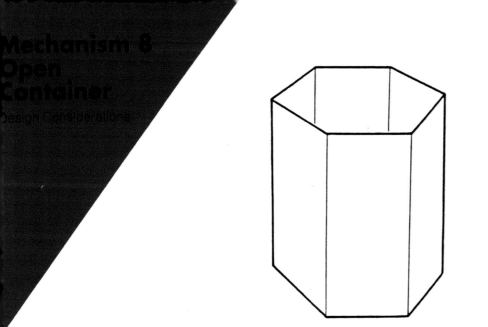

For a container to have as large a capacity as possible, the elastic band and the floor need to be near the bottom. This can cause some distortion at the top and suggests that it should be possible to design a container where the top is larger than the bottom.

In business to business advertising there is a pressing need to think of devices which will keep the sender's name in front of a customer for as long as possible. Hence the great number of calendars and diaries which are sent out each year. This mechanism falls into this category because it could be used as a pen and pencil holder and it might remain on the customer's desk all year. Its novelty attracts attention initially, and its usefulness keeps it here.

A hexagon is probably the most pleasing shape for hollow containers, but it is also interesting to experiment with other cross-sections such as squares, pentagons, heptagons and octagons. Each presents its own challenge and offers different possibilities. The top edges do not have to be straight. Try shaping them to add variety to your design.

If one pencil holder seems a good idea, perhaps a nest of pencil holders is an even better one. It is an interesting design problem to link these shapes to make a pleasing group and to arrange it so that they all collapse flat. One obvious thought is that all the elastic bands should be parallel.

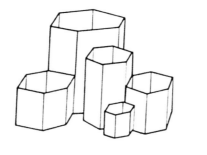

The ultimate design of this kind would be an up-pop cylinder. To make it curve satisfactorily it needs to have as many folds as possible. This weakens the sides so that the elastic band has to run from end to end, making it a closed container. In fact, more akin to mechanism 9 rather than mechanism 8. It is a tricky mechanism to make well and do not expect too much from it.

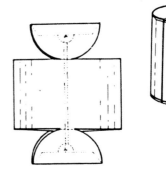

Such models will normally have the elastic bands exposed and visible underneath, but it is a simple matter to construct an extra floor to hide them, if that is thought desirable.

Mechanism 9
Right Prism

A right prism is one where the end planes are at right angles to its edges. When it is released this up-pop jumps rapidly into a shape which has surprising solidity. Once the principles of this mechanism are understood it becomes a simple matter to design other right prisms with different cross-sections, both regular and irregular.

▲ ▲

GLUE BAND FOR MECHANISM 9 HERE.

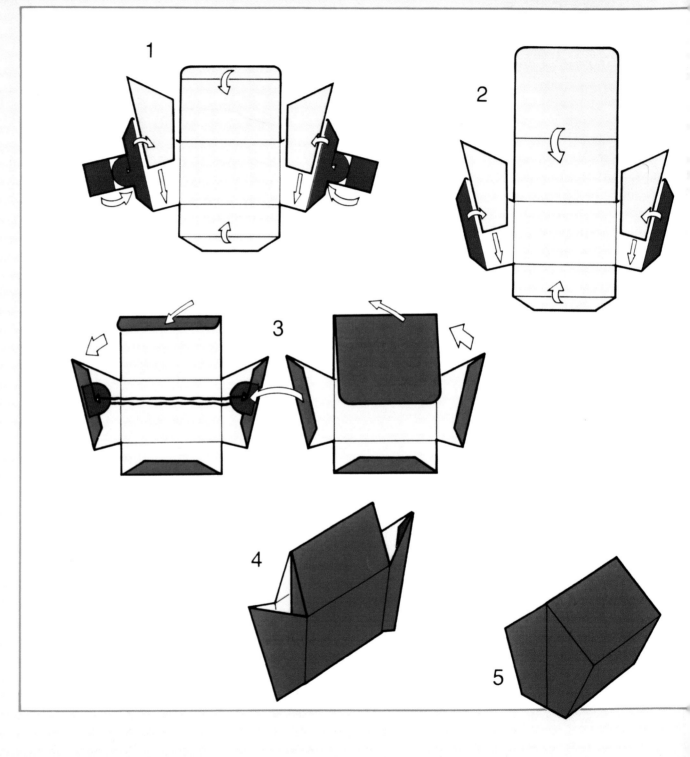

Mechanism 10 Signal Arms

Just as black and white images stand out when everything else is in colour, so this essentially two-dimensional motion offers a new surprise in an art where three-dimensional shapes are the norm. It is a mechanism with great possibilities for development and imaginative design.

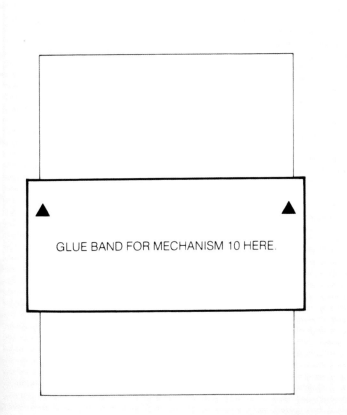

GLUE BAND FOR MECHANISM 10 HERE.

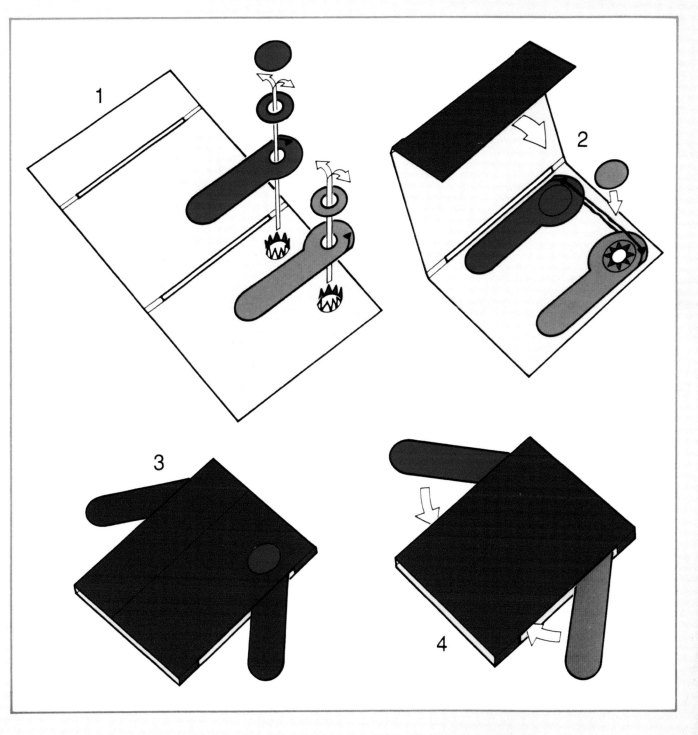

1

2

3

4

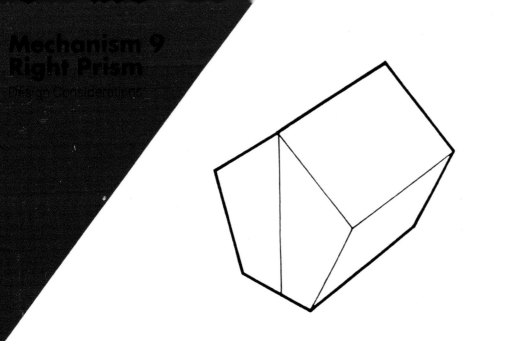

This is a mechanism where the concept is an easy one, but where practical paper engineering knowledge is needed if it is to work well. The ends must pull flat, but not collapse inwards and so there has to be a "stop" in the form of a piece of card which stretches the full length of the prism. The pressure of the elastic can also cause the ends to buckle and so it is a wise precaution to double the thickness of the material there. This is preferable to using double thickness material throughout and so making the whole model too clumsy.

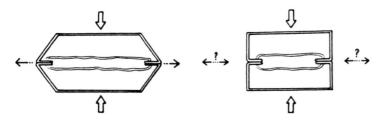

When a concave shape is squashed, the sides have no option but to fold outwards, but a shape which has its sides at 90° could fold either outwards or inwards and so it might need help to start it off. It is not necessarily a fault in a mechanism if it is a little difficult to flatten, because some devices only need to up-pop once successfully to achieve their surprise effect.

This mechanism lends itself to making a most appealing little up-pop house, especially if it is carefully decorated. Note how chimneys may be added to the end walls without interfering with the mechanism and how the glue flap can become part of the ridge design if it is glued to the outside. It might, however, be better to glue this flap inside and then make an extra v-shaped piece out of thinner paper to form a double-ridge detail.

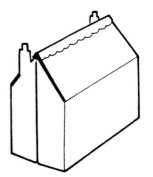

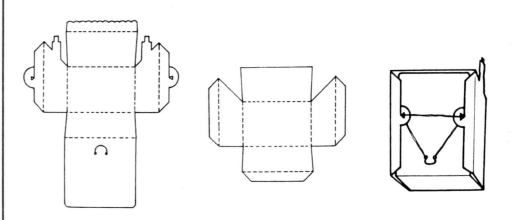

The net of this house also shows a further interesting feature. There is a third hook on the central separating card. The elastic band then forms a triangle and pulls it all into shape rather more neatly.